Many of the local people, the Britons, were forced to move west or north into Wales, Scotland and Cornwall.

At first the Anglo-Saxons lived in small groups of a few families. Then people began to live in bigger groups for safety. These groups became tribes with a **chieftain** as their leader.

These tribes began to join together in even bigger groups and their leaders were called kings. There were five Anglo-Saxon kingdoms.

The Anglo-Saxon kingdoms

Build a house

Roman buildings were made of stone or brick with tiled roofs. The Anglo-Saxons didn't like these big buildings. They built their own homes and left the Roman ones to fall down.

Anglo-Saxon houses were made of wood. The roof was **thatched** with reeds or straw. The doors and windows faced south, as this was the best way to catch heat and light from the sun.

bed covers of wool or animal skin

There were no comforts like carpets, sofas or electricity. Houses were furnished with simple wooden furniture – beds and stools or benches. There were boxes to store things like food and blankets, and valuable items were kept in chests with locks. Houses could get quite crowded as the whole family slept in one room, which could mean 10 or 12 people.

A firebox was made of wood and lined with clay. The fire heated the house and gave some light.

high wooden fence to keep out wild animals like wolves

STAGE 3

Throw a party

Each town or village usually had a hall – a big building where everyone could gather. There was feasting, music, singing, games and dancing. **Acrobats** showed their skill and strength and people told stories, poems and riddles.

roast pig →

drinking cup (cow's horn)

mead (drink made from → honey)

board game

6

Do something useful

The Anglo-Saxons liked to own beautiful things. If you were a **craftsman** you made them out of wood, clay, stone and metal. Lumps of clay were dug out of the ground and left in a pond to become soft. The clay was rolled into long strips which were wound round and round to make pots.

The clay was smoothed down. ↓

Little stamps were pressed into the clay to make patterns. ↙

The pot was baked hard in a bonfire covered in turf. ↘

If you weren't a craftsman, you might have been a farmer. Farmers grew wheat in their fields and this was used to make bread. They kept cattle, sheep, goats and pigs. These animals gave meat and milk to turn into butter and cheese. Their skins were turned into leather clothes, shoes and bags. Eggs came from chickens, geese and ducks and fish were caught in the rivers.

workshop

fishing in the river

hen house

fence and basket made of woven willow

scaring off birds with a sling shot

sowing seeds

Try on a tunic

If you were an Anglo-Saxon woman you spent a lot of your time spinning and **weaving**. Thread was spun from sheep and goat hair and was woven into cloth on a **loom**. Then the cloth was made into clothes.

Most people wore a tunic like a shirt. It could be long or short and was usually pulled in at the waist with a leather belt. Many poor people went barefoot.

⊂ clay weights
to keep
the threads taut

lady's tunic
with braids
on hems ↙

← chain with keys,
scissors, nail
clippers and
other handy
things

Men wore trousers
or leggings held
in place with strips
of cloth.

woollen cap

cloak for wet
weather pinned
with brooch

purse

leather shoes
with buckles

Wealthy people owned things decorated with gold, silver
and precious stones. A man showed how important he was
by carrying a beautiful sword.

Wealthy women wore veils
of silk and fabulous jewellery.
They made ringlets in their hair
with curling tongs and grew
their nails long.

11

STAGE
6

Know who you are

In Anglo-Saxon times, some people were very wealthy and some were very poor. The king and queen were the richest and most powerful people in the kingdom. People who worked for the king became rich as well.

If you were an ealdorman, you were the king's **deputy** and you gave him advice when he needed help. You had to provide soldiers if the king went into battle. Ealdormen owned lots of land.

an ealdorman hunting with a hawk and hounds

If you were a reeve you did a lot of work for the king. You might collect **taxes** or look after a town or a large area of land.

If you were a carl you worked on the land and owned one or two farms. A carl was not as rich as a reeve. If he made enough money to build a big house he could become a reeve.

If you were a non-freeman or slave you had to work for someone else. However, you got paid for work so you might be able to save up and buy your freedom.

↑ A port reeve checked for ships.

a carl →

slaves working for the carl ↓

Speak to a god

By the time the Romans left Britain in 400 CE, some people had changed their religion from pagan to Christian. When the Anglo-Saxons settled, they brought back the pagan religion.

Anglo-Saxons were known as pagans because they prayed to lots of gods. People went to a special place – perhaps a clearing in a wood – and left gifts for their gods. They hoped the gods would then protect them.

People left gifts of food and drink – or even dead animals – for the gods.

There were special spells you could use to protect your crops from wicked elves – like dropping a little honey, milk or oil round your field.

If you were an Anglo-Saxon, perhaps you prayed to one of these gods. Some days of the week are named after Anglo-Saxon gods.

Tiw
god of war
Tuesday

Woden
leader of the gods
Wednesday

Thor
god of thunder
Thursday

Frija
Woden's wife
Friday

Eostre was another Anglo-Saxon goddess. People believed she brought the flowers and put leaves on the trees in Spring. The word Easter comes from her name.

Become a Christian again

If you were an Anglo-Saxon in the kingdom of Kent,
you might have seen a group of strangers arrive one day.
Their leader was called Augustine and he had come from
Rome to persuade King Ethelbert to become a Christian.

Just as Augustine was about to enter Kent, he lost his courage.

Er... I think we'll come back another day.

He went all the way back to Rome but the head of the church, the Pope, wasn't pleased.

It's your duty to do this, my son.

Augustine went back to Kent again.

Right, this time I'll do it!

Ethelbert listened to what Augustine had to say and then agreed to become a Christian. If a king changed his religion, the people of his kingdom usually changed their religion, too. After that, Christianity spread through the rest of England.

Ethelbert gave Augustine permission to build a **monastery** outside the town of Canterbury. Other people began to build churches and because they were important buildings, they were often built of stone rather than wood.

Live in a monastery

If you were an Anglo-Saxon who wanted more time to worship the Christian God, you became a monk or a nun.

Monks lived in a monastery. They spent a lot of their day singing and praying in their church. If other people wanted the monks to pray for them they gave a gift to the monastery — money, a piece of land or a cow.

church

monks' houses

guest house

refectory (dining hall) and kitchen

vegetable garden

hospital

18

The monks did other things as well. It was the monks in the monasteries who did most of the writing and teaching. They cared for the sick and dying and gave shelter to travellers. They worked on their farms to provide food for the people in the monastery.

making medicines from herbs

teaching children to read

building new houses

giving food to the poor

orchard

meeting and writing house

fields

19

Fight a Viking

When merchants came to
England in ships with goods
to sell they had to pay tax
on the things they brought.
If you were a reeve who collected
taxes, you had to keep a lookout
for these ships.

Nice piece
of land
you've got
here!

One day around 700 CE, a ship arrived
which was not a merchant ship but
a **longship** full of Vikings. They had
not come to sell things but to
raid England.

The Viking raids went on for years.
The Anglo-Saxons paid the Vikings
to go away but they kept coming back.
They took over Anglo-Saxon farms
and settled down. Soon, all of England
except the Kingdom of Wessex
belonged to the Vikings.

Alfred was King of Wessex and fought many battles to try and force the Vikings out of England.

One Christmas, the Vikings made a surprise attack on Alfred's fort and he had to escape. He hid in the marshes of the west of England while he made plans.

Alfred gathered together an army and marched towards the Viking lands. This time he won the battle and Guthrum, King of the Vikings, was defeated. Guthrum agreed to become a Christian like Alfred.

In return, the Vikings were allowed to stay and keep their own laws and **customs**. Their part of the country became known as the Danelaw.

Make a book

Most Anglo-Saxons couldn't read or write, so they had to remember events and stories from their lives and tell them to other people before they died so they weren't forgotten. However, over the years, some were forgotten or mistakes were made.

This is why King Alfred knew it would be good for the kingdom if more people could read. He set up schools where children, rich or poor, could be taught. He made sure that everything that happened in the kingdom was written down.

A monk called Bede lived in a monastery at Jarrow in the north of England. He was the first person to write a history of England.

pen made from a goose feather (quill)

knife to keep the quill sharp

People wrote on pieces of animal skin called vellum or parchment. A lot of things had to be done to the skins before you could write on them.

Preparing vellum

1 Soak the animal skins in water — cow and calf skins are best. It's easier to scrape off the hair once the skin has been soaked for a while.

2 Stretch a skin on a wooden frame to dry.

3 Don't use nails to stretch the skin as they will tear it. Instead...

...press a round pebble into the skin and fasten it with a piece of cord. Scrape it until it is clean and thin.

4 Cut the vellum into rectangles then sew the pages together to make a book.

Take something with you

When Anglo-Saxons died they were buried and sometimes the grave was marked with a wooden post. Some of the dead person's possessions were put into the grave, too, in case the person needed them in another life. If you were a poor Anglo-Saxon there might be things like a pot, a small knife or a string of beads.

If you were a rich Anglo-Saxon man, a sword, helmet, spear and shield might be put into the grave. A rich woman might be buried with her gold jewellery – or perhaps a pair of tweezers! Sometimes food was put into the grave like eggs, nuts, fruit – or even a cooked **lobster**. The things in the grave showed how important the person was.

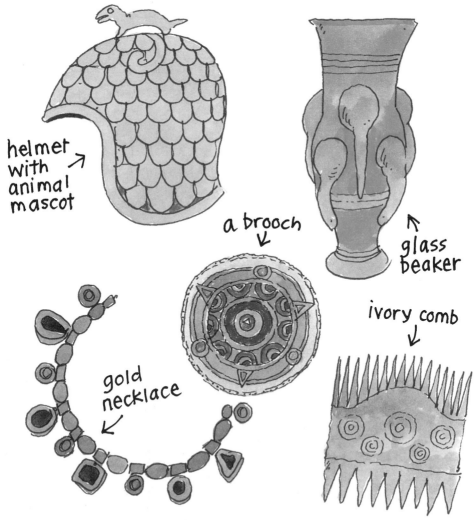

helmet with animal mascot ↗

a brooch ↓

glass beaker ↖

ivory comb ↓

gold necklace ↙

See the Normans arrive

Anglo-Saxon kings had trouble keeping the kingdom peaceful and there was often fighting between the Anglo-Saxons and the Vikings. They all wanted to protect their own lands and perhaps take some land from someone else.

A man called Edward the Confessor was the thirteenth Anglo-Saxon king. He had no children so when he died his brother-in-law, Harold, Earl Godwin, was chosen as the next king.

This didn't please William, Duke of Normandy, because William claimed that Edward the Confessor had promised *he* would be the next king. So he came across the channel from Normandy to fight Harold for his kingdom.

If you lived on the south coast of England in 1066 you would have seen a huge fleet of ships arriving with William's army. Harold's soldiers were ready to fight for their king with battleaxes, swords and shields. However, William's archers sent a great shower of arrows into Harold's army. Harold was killed and his army defeated. Duke William – known as William the Conqueror – was now king of England.

The Normans had arrived and the Anglo-Saxon times were over. Could you have lived as an Anglo-Saxon?

Glossary

acrobats people who do difficult and exciting tricks, such as standing on their hands

chieftain the leader of a tribe

craftsman someone who uses a lot of skill to make things

customs ways of doing things that are special to a group of people

deputy second-in-command; someone who has been given the right to act in place of a more important person

invaded entered a country by force

lobster a sea-creature with eight legs and a pair of sharp claws

longship a narrow wooden ship with oars and a square sail, used by the Vikings

loom a wooden frame on which cloth can be woven

monastery a special building where people can spend their lives worshipping the Christian God

raid a sudden attack by an enemy, who wants to take your possessions

Roman Empire all the lands ruled by the Ancient Romans

settled came to live permanently; set up home

taxes the part of a person's earnings that they have to give to the government each year

thatched covered in dried reeds or straw that act as a roof

weaving making cloth

Index

Anglo-Saxon timeline

Romans

Anglo-Saxo

Arrived
55 BCE...

...left
400 CE

Most Anglo-Saxons
settled in Britain
by 450 CE

Vikings

Invaded
700 CE

Normans

Invaded
1066 CE

31

Ideas for reading

Written by Linda Pagett B.Ed (hons), M.Ed
Lecturer and Educational Consultant

Learning objectives: use syntax, context and word structure to build store of vocabulary as they read for meaning; identify and make notes of the main points of sections of text; present information, ensuring relevant details are included; use some drama strategies to explore issues

Curriculum links: Why have people invaded and settled in Britain in the past? An Anglo-Saxon case study

Interest words: acrobat, carl, ealdorman, firebox, fort, kingdom, longship, lyre, mead, monastery, monks, pagans, raid, reeve, roman empire, sling shot, vellum, willow

Resources: whiteboard, globe, writing materials

Getting started

This book can be read over two or more guided reading sessions.

- Look at the cover together and invite one of the children to read the blurb. Discuss as a group what the 13 stages may entail.

- Compile a list of key questions that children have about the Anglo-Saxons and write them on the whiteboard.

Reading and responding

- Read pp2–3 together and find Denmark, Germany and the Netherlands on a globe. Check that children understand why the Angles and Saxons invaded.

- Turn to the contents page and, in pairs, give children a few stages each to read, ensuring the whole book is covered. Demonstrate how to make very simple notes using only one or two words to record points.

- Support weaker readers; remind children to read for meaning when they come across tricky words, asking themselves, *Does this make sense?*